THE MENTAL EQUIVALENT

STUDY

WORKBOOK

Adapted from Emmet Fox's

Landmark classic The Mental Equivalent
by Stein Koraki

COPYRIGHT NOTICE

The Mental Equivalent| Workbook

CONTENT

If a child could be taught only one thing, it should be taught that this is a mental world, and to know that is the key to life.

UNIVERSAL POLARITY

Go where you like, seek where you will, you find the Trinity

UNIVERSAL POLARITY

Answer the following questions below as best as you can. If you find it difficult answering some of the questions, go back and reread the book on the chapter. It's important that you have a full understanding of the key concepts.

What is the law of Polarity?

What is the law of Polarity equivalent to in the organic world?

What is the real ultimate meaning behind the Trinity?

What two factors lead to demonstration? What is "Feeling" in connection with thought?

How do you remove negative thoughts from your mind?

What is the law of mind?

How do you build a mental equivalent of happiness and prosperity?

Complete the following sentences below

Father, mother, child: Activity, material,

You build a mental equivalent for what you want by getting

Complete the following sentences below

The right though automatically expunges the

In your own words and understanding, explain the key to the management of your mind?

NOTES

BUILDING A NEW MENTAL EQUIVALENT

You must change your thought and keep it changed

BUILDING A NEW MENTAL EQUIVALENT

Answer the following questions below as best as you can. If you find it difficult answering some of the questions, go back and reread the book on the chapter. It's important that you have a full understanding of the key concepts.

Why are we here on earth?

Why is it necessary to demonstrate the law of being?

What is the secret of controlling your life?

What is the secret of accomplishment?

What is the secret of harmony and success?

Complete the following sentences below

Harmonious thoughts mean

Fear thought or anger thought means

In your own words, explain the analogy of the photographic camera in relation to focus?

NOTES

MAINTAINING THE NEW EQUIVALENT

There is no truth in our seeming troubles. There is no reality in lack.

MAINTAINING THE NEW EQUIVALENT

Answer the following questions below as best as you can. If you find it difficult answering some of the questions, go back and reread the book on the chapter. It's important that you have a full understanding of the key concepts.

Why must you "act the part" in respect to changing your condition?

How does the inner condition relate to the outer projection of action?

What is a true action?

What is a false action?

What is the great enemy of prayer?

Exercise

In your own words, explain the relationship between captivity and false beliefs. Give three examples.

NOTES